PowerPoint 2010
Foundation to Intermediate Guide

Chris Voyse and Patrice Muse

Published by
Voyse Recognition Limited

Smart PC Guides • Century Business Centre • Manvers Way • Manvers
Rotherham • South Yorkshire • S63 5DA • 01709 300188
www.smart-pc-guides.com

© 2010 Voyse Recognition Limited

This guide has been designed in order to create a methodical approach to learning this product. www.smart-pc-guides.com outlines all the guides in the Office 2010 portfolio.

Notice of Liability

First Published in Great Britain in 2010

Voyse Recognition Limited
Smart PC Guides
Century Business Centre
Manvers Way
Manvers
Rotherham
South Yorkshire
S63 5DA
01709 300188

ISBN 978 1 905657 476

Foundation to Intermediate Objectives

Page

Table of Contents

Introducing PowerPoint

PowerPoint 2010 is an application that enables slides to be generated, edited and presented to either an individual or group of users. Notes pages can be generated to enhance the presentation, handouts can be produced and PowerPoint offers a variety of printing options.

Opening PowerPoint

There are several ways that this application can be opened. To open the PowerPoint 2010 application, select the Start Button [image], move the mouse pointer ᴋ and pause over ▶ All Programs , click with the left 🖱 button on Microsoft Office ; select P Microsoft PowerPoint 2010 , click with the left 🖱 button to open the programme.

Tour of the Screen

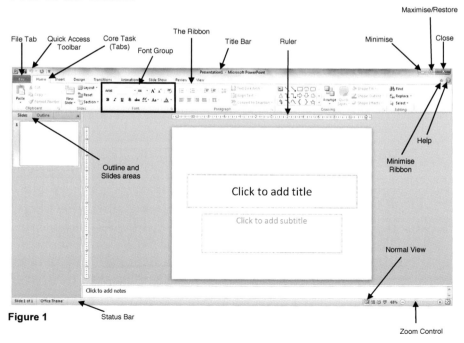

Figure 1

File Tab

In PowerPoint 2010 the File Tab replaces the office button and the file menu found in previous versions of PowerPoint and displays the commands for Save, Save As, Open, Close, Info, Recent, New, Print, Save and Send, Help, Options and Exit and the related options available under each command.

Quick Access Toolbar

The Quick Access Toolbar can be found in the top section of the screen. It allows the user to display commands that are regularly used and that are independent of their associated tabs. There is the option to locate the Quick Access Toolbar in two locations near to the top section of the screen.

Title Bar

The Title Bar is highlighted in black and defines the name of the application that the user is in and the name of the presentation open. PowerPoint will automatically display the default name, for example Presentation1, however, once the presentation has been saved the name of the saved presentation will be displayed in this area.

Ribbon

The Ribbon is the control centre to quickly help find the commands that help the user to complete a task. The Ribbon is organised into three parts

Core Tasks: consisting of seven Tabs: Home, Insert, Design, Animations, Slide Show, Review and View

Groups: related items grouped together

Commands: buttons, boxes and menus that give instruction

The Ribbon organises the commands into logical groups all collected together under the Tabs with each Tab relating to a type of activity. Some Tabs only appear when they are needed whilst others are visible all the time.

To minimise the Ribbon double click with the left button on the active Tab, for example Design, the Ribbon and its commands disappear. To display the Ribbon and its commands, click with the left button on the Tab. Alternatively press CTRL F1 to collapse or expand the Tabs.

Help Icon

The Help icon can be found on the Ribbon or by pressing F1

Scroll Bars

Horizontal and Vertical scroll bars enable users to move around the presentation.

Zoom Control

To use the Zoom Control drag with the left button to increase (magnify) or decrease the presentation to display the information larger or smaller on the screen.

Status Bar

The Status Bar is at the bottom of the screen, to customise the Status Bar

1. Right click on the Status Bar, the Customise Status Bar appears
2. To activate the View Indicator to be displayed in the Status Bar
3. Click with the left button on <u>View Indicator</u>
4. A tick ✓ is displayed to indicate the feature has been activated
5. Click back in the presentation
6. Slide 1 of 1 is displayed in the Status Bar to show that the View Indicated is activated

The Status Bar also tells the user which theme has been applied to the selected slide "Office Theme"

Notes Page

Notes Page displays a reduced image of the slide; it also allows the user to edit any notes before printing them out.

Normal View

The Normal View icon is on the left hand side of the Status Bar or is activated by selecting View , Normal from the Ribbon.

Slide Sorter View

The Sorter View icon is found on the Status Bar or is activated by selecting View , Slide Sorter from the Ribbon. This displays all the slides within a presentation. Slides can be moved or copied and slide transition effects displayed and added from here for an onscreen slide show.

Slide Show

The Slide Show can be displayed by selecting the Slide Show icon that is located on the Status Bar or is activated by selecting Slide Show from the Ribbon.

Note: If you are working in Windows XP instead of Windows Vista or Windows 7, dialog boxes may look different but function in a similar way.

Methodology of Creating Presentations

A presentation is a means of communicating information to an audience in a clear and effective manner using a variety of output media.

Preparation Work

How will the presentation be delivered to the audience?

- With a computer using a projector
- On a standalone computer
- Simple slide show
- Stand up presentation
- Use of acetates or an overhead projector
- Use of handouts
- Do corporate colours and font styles need to be included in the presentation?
- What graphics are to be used in the presentation?
- Does the presentation require use of transitions?
- Are Header and Footer areas required?
- What type of Background is required?

Page Setup

PowerPoint displays the default design for a title slide; however this can be changed by using Page Setup.

1. Select

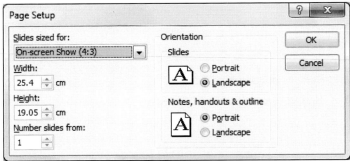

Figure 2

2. In the **S**lides sized for: area, the default is set as On-screen Show

3. Choose the ▾ to view alternative options

4.   Choose the orientation settings for Slides and Notes, handouts and outline

5.   Press [OK]

Figure 3

1.   PowerPoint displays the default themes available from the Themes Grouping

2.   The Themes Grouping contains built in [Colors ▾], [A] Fonts ▾ and [◯] Effects ▾

3.   Click with the left 🖱 button on the downward pointing arrow to extend the Themes menu

Defining the Background Colour

The type of presentation will determine the choice of background.

1.   Select the [Design] Tab, click with the left 🖱 button on [Background Styles ▾]

2.   The following gallery appears

Figure 4

3.   Move over any of the styles to display the theme colours in the presentation

4.   Click with the left 🖱 button on [Format Background...]

5.   The Format Background dialog box is displayed

Figure 5

6. Select the Colour icon 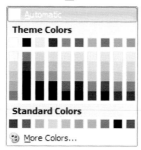 to expand the menu

Figure 6

7. Select a Theme Colour, the slide changes to show the chosen colour

8. Press Reset Background , the slide changes back to the default slide colour

9. Re-select the <u>C</u>olour icon, choose More Colors...

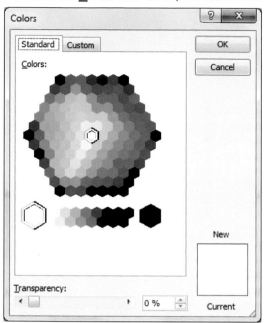

Figure 7

10. The Standard colours are displayed, select the Custom Tab

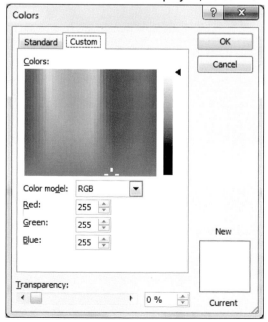

Figure 8

11. Select a colour to be used in the presentation

12. To lighten or darken the colour use the black marker ◀

13. Select [OK]

Figure 9

14. Select <u>T</u>ransparency, adjust the transparency to 72%

15. Press [Apply to All]

16. The background colour is applied to all the slides in the presentation

Fill Effects

1. Choose [Design], select [Background Styles ▾], choose [Format Background...]

2. The Format Background dialog box appears

3. Click on the **G**radient fill, select [Preset colors: ☐ ▾]

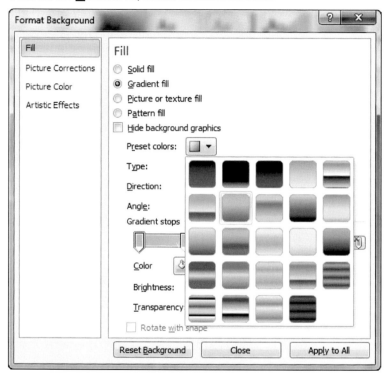

Figure 10

4. The P**re**-set colour pallet is displayed

5. Select the colour Ocean, choose [Direction: ☐ ▾], select Linear Up

Figure 11

6. The Directional options change with each shading style

7. To adjust the gradient, click and drag the stop buttons

8. Click with the left button to Add a Gradient Stop

9. Click with the left button to Delete a Gradient Stop

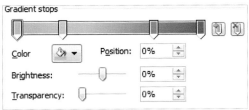

Figure 12

10. Select Apply to All , click Close

11. The fill effect is applied to all the slides in the presentation

Picture and Texture Effects

1. Choose [Design], select [Background Styles ▾], choose
   [Format Background...]

2. The Format Background dialog box appears

3. Press with the left 🖰 button on [◉ Picture or texture fill]

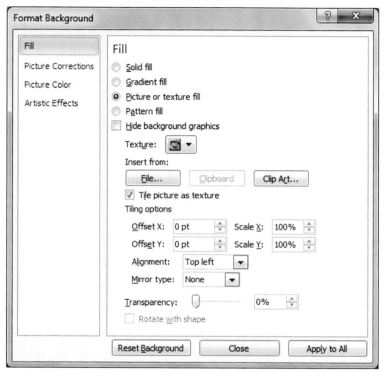

Figure 13

4. Select the Texture icon, choose Water Droplets

5. Use the [Transparency: ——○—— 55% ▴▾] slide ruler to adjust the texture

6. Alternatively click [File...] to move to the Sample Pictures area

7. Select the required picture, click [Insert ▾]

8. Choose [Clip Art...] to select a piece of clipart as a background

9. [Apply to All] applies the picture or textured effect to all the slides

10. Select [Close]

Bullets and Numbering

PowerPoint can create text to appear on different levels using different font styles and colours.

Title and Content

1. Select Home , Layout ▾ , choose

2. In the Click to add title area type Using Bullets

3. In the Click to add text area type Level 1, press Enter to move to the next bullet

4. To indent the bullet and text to the next level, select Increase List Level icon from the Paragraph Grouping

5. Type Level 2, repeat steps 4 and 5, type Level 3

6. Continue the process until five levels have been generated

7. To move back a level, click the left button on the level to be changed

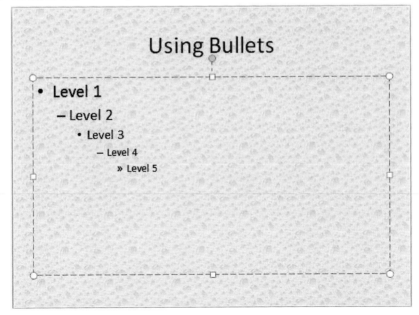

Figure 14

8. Select the Decrease List Level icon to move back to the required level

Formatting Bullets

1. Select the bullet(s) to be formatted
2. Click on the downward pointing arrow on the Bullets icon ⬛ from the Paragraph Grouping

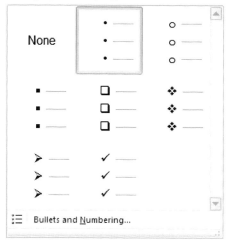

Figure 15

3. Select ⬛ Bullets and Numbering...
4. The Bullets and Numbering dialog box appears

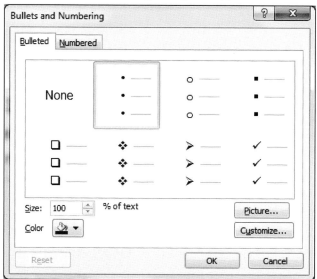

Figure 16

5. Adjust the size as required `Size: 100 [↕] % of text`

6. Choose `Color [◇▼]` to define the required colour

7. Click `Customize...`, select the font Wingdings

8. Use the scroll bars to view the different bullet styles

9. Select a graphical style required for the bullet

10. Press `OK` twice to return to the presentation

11. The selected bullet style is applied

12. Select `View`, `[✔] Ruler` to display the ruler

13. Press `ALT` `W` `R` to show or hide the ruler

14. The 🔺 icon is used to increase the distanced from the bullet

15. The ▽ icon enables the bullet to be moved nearer to the text

16. To move bullet and text together, click and drag the left button on the ▭ icon

Saving a Presentation

1. Select `File`, `Save As`

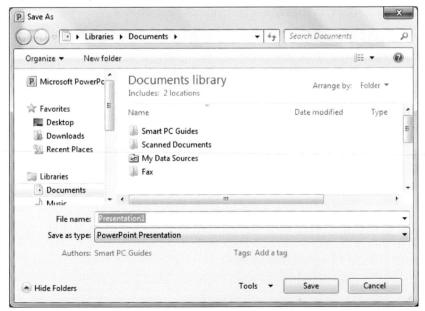

Figure 17

2. Alternatively press [F12] to display the Save As dialog box

3. In the File name area save the presentation as Using Bullets

4. In the Save as type area the default is set to save items as a PowerPoint Presentation

5. Select [Save]

6. The title bar area displays the named presentation

Note: If a user requires to save, open or work in a presentation in a previous version, click on the downward arrow ▼ in the Save as type dialog box and select, PowerPoint 97-2003 Presentation, click Save. The Compatibility Checker may appear if features in 2010 have been used that are not available in previous versions. In 2010 the Title bar will state [Compatibility Mode] identifying that the presentation is not saved in a 2010 format.

Save a Presentation as a PDF

A presentation can be saved as a PDF (Portable Document Format); that is a fixed layout format and is a useful method of saving a presentation that is intended to be read and printed but not modified. To read a PDF the user will need to have Acrobat Reader installed on the computer.

1. Select [File], [Save As]

2. In the File name box type Using Bullets

3. The Save as type area defaults as a PowerPoint Presentation

4. Using the arrow key scroll down and select PDF

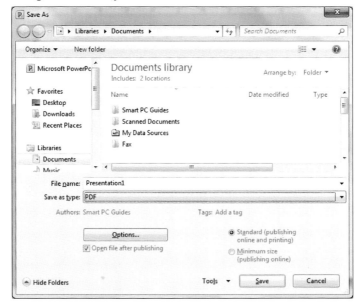

Figure 18

5. Choose Optimise for: select Standard (publishing online and printing)
6. Click with the left  button on [Options...]
7. Select the required options

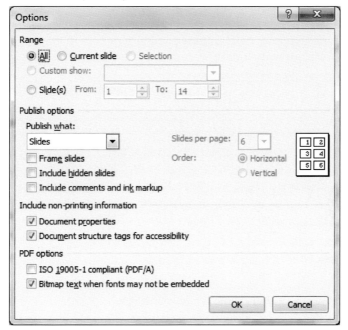

Figure 19

8. Click [OK], select [Save]
9. The presentation is displayed as a PDF that can be read and printed but not modified

Adding a New Slide to a Presentation

1. Select [Home]

2. Click on the downward pointing arrow on the New Slide icon
3. Alternatively press [ALT] [H] [I]
4. Choose the required layout

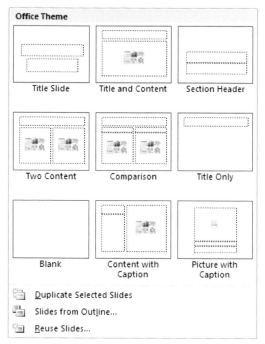

Figure 20

5. To change the layout of the slide, re-select the slide

6. Choose [📋 Layout ▾] and select the new layout

Creating Headers and Footers

1. Select Insert, Header & Footer, the Header and Footer dialog box appears

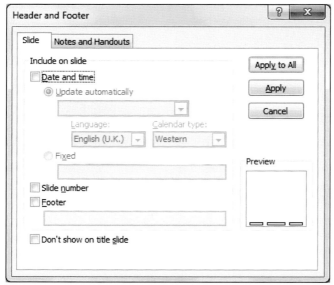

Figure 21

2. Select <u>D</u>ate and time, choose <u>U</u>pdate automatically

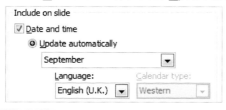

Figure 22

3. Or select Fi<u>x</u>ed, type in the date required

4. Tick ☑ Slide number to identify a slide by a number

5. Click in the <u>F</u>ooter area, type the required information

6. Apply to All applies the Header and Footer information to all the Slides

7. Apply inserts the information to an individual slide

8. Select ☑ Don't show on title slide if information is not to be displayed

Exercise 1: - Create a Simple Presentation

1. Open a new presentation
2. In the Click to add title, type Working with PowerPoint
3. In the Click to add subtitle, type your name
4. Add a coloured background or texture of your choice

Two Content

5. Add the new slide named
6. Ensure the ruler is displayed, create the following slide

Working with Five Levels

❑Level 1	❑ Level 1
❑Level 2	❑ Level 2
❑Level 3	❑ Level 3
❑Level 4	❑ Level 4
❑Level 5	❑ Level 5

7. Choose a style of bullet and display the five levels in the left column
8. Highlight the five levels, change the font size to 32
9. In the right column display five bullets at Level 1
10. In the right column click on the ▽ triangle and drag to 2
11. Use the ruler marker triangle 🛆 to increase the spacing from the bullet
12. Add a new slide Title Only, add the title Working with Shapes
13. Save the presentation as Creating My First Presentation
14. Close the presentation

Inserting Shapes

1. Open a new presentation

2. Select **File** , **New** , **Blank presentation**

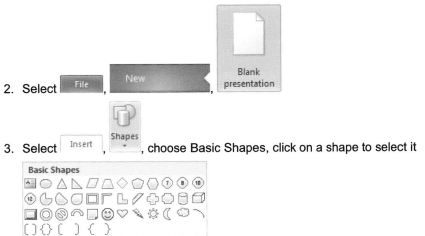

3. Select **Insert** , **Shapes** , choose Basic Shapes, click on a shape to select it

Figure 23

4. Move the mouse pointer ⬚ onto the blank slide

5. Click and drag with the left ⬚ button to insert the shape

6. Repeat the process to add three additional

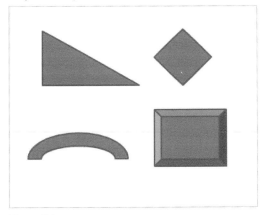

Figure 24

7. Click and drag the shapes to move them to different locations on the slide

Change Default Colour

1. Click on the select shape with the right ⌐𝖇 button

2. Select 🖌 Format Shape...

3. The Format Shape dialog box appears

Figure 25

4. To change the fill colour, select ⊙ Solid fill , Color: 🖌 ▾

5. To lighten or darken a selected colour, adjust Transparency to the required shade

Figure 26

6. To change the colour and weight of lines, select Line Color

7. To change the line style, select Line Style , choose the required options

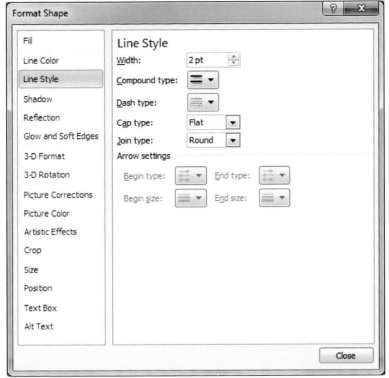

Figure 27

8. Choose Close to view the changes to the slide, save the changes

AutoShape Defaults

1. Move the mouse pointer ↖ over the shape with the new default settings
2. Click with the right 🖱 button on the shape, choose Set as Default Shape
3. Select a shape from the basic shapes gallery
4. Click the left 🖱 button to display the shape with the new default settings
5. To revert to the original default setting
6. Move the mouse pointer ↖ over the shape, click with the right 🖱 button
7. Select Format Shape... , choose the original settings, click Close
8. Move the mouse pointer ↖ over the shape with the new default settings
9. Click with the right 🖱 button on the shape, choose Set as Default Shape

Undo and Redo

PowerPoint enables a user to enter text in a presentation and store that information in its memory allowing the user to go backwards or forwards on a step by step basis. The Undo and Redo icons can be found on the Quick Access Toolbar located at the top left of the screen.

To Amend the Undo Default Settings

1. Select **File** , **Options** , **Advanced**

PowerPoint Options

General
Proofing
Save
Language
Advanced
Customize Ribbon
Quick Access Toolbar
Add-Ins
Trust Center

Advanced options for working with PowerPoint.

Editing options

☑ When selecting, automatically select entire word
☑ Allow text to be dragged and dropped
Maximum number of undos: 20

Cut, copy, and paste

☑ Use smart cut and paste
☑ Show Paste Options button when content is pasted

Image Size and Quality   Presentation1 ▾

☐ Discard editing data
☐ Do not compress images in file
Set default target output to: 220 ppi ▾

Display

Show this number of Recent Documents: 25
☑ Show shortcut keys in ScreenTips
☑ Show vertical ruler
☐ Disable hardware graphics acceleration

OK   Cancel

Figure 28

2. Select Editing options

3. Change the Maximum number of undo's to 150

4.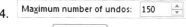

5. Press OK

Gridlines

When using drawing objects, gridlines can be switched on to help with accurate positioning of an object.

1. Select View , ✓ Gridlines , alternatively press ALT V I

2. The Grid and Guides dialog box appears

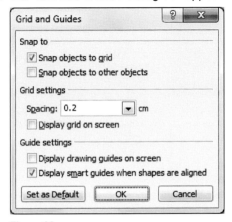

Figure 29

3. Choose ✓ Snap objects to grid and ✓ Display grid on screen , click OK

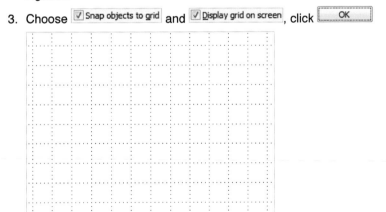

Figure 30

4. Grid lines appear on the slide in the screen as vertical and horizontal lines

5. Select ALT V I , deselect the required tick to switch off the gridlines

6. Press OK to return to the presentation

Spell Check Facility

1. Select , , alternatively press F7

2. The Spell Checker will spell check the presentation or selected text

3. Words that are not recognised in the dictionary are highlighted

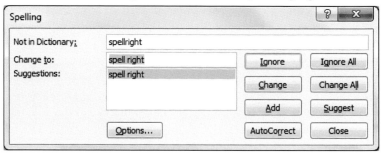

Figure 31

4. The dialog box highlights any applicable suggestions, select Ignore or Change

5. Add adds the word to the dictionary

6. Choose Ignore All to ignore all suggestions from the spell checker

7. Select Change All to change all corrections suggested from the spell checker

Working with the Slide Master

With the Slide Master a theme can be set for a presentation using font styles, background colours and company logos. Once created the attributes from the Slide Master are applied to the new slide, if selected the Slide Master incorporates the same identity to all the slides saving development time. If a date and time is applied for example, the Slide Master uses these settings for the entire presentation.

View Slide Master

1. Select , or press [ALT] [W] [M]

2. This displays the Master Title style

3. Alternatively move the mouse pointer ⌖ over Normal View 🞖

4. Hold down the [SHIFT] key, double click with the left 🖰 button

5. The following screen appears

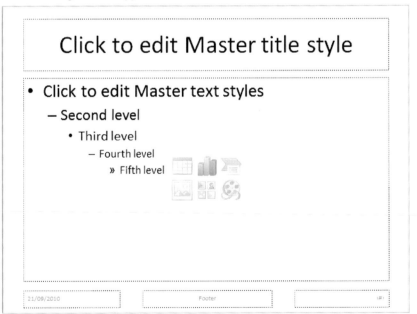

Figure 32

Changing the Date and Time Settings

1. Highlight the date/time, select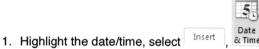

2. Select the required format

3. Choose Default...

4. The following prompt appears

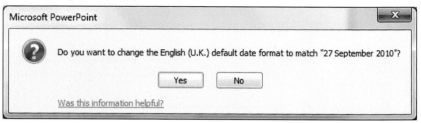

Figure 33

5. Click Yes

6. Press OK to apply the format to the presentation

Inserting the Date and Time

1. Click on the Date placeholder in the bottom left hand corner of the Slide Master

2. Select Insert , Header & Footer

3. The Header and Footer dialog box appears

4. Click with the left 👆 button in the **D**ate and time, a tick ☑ is displayed

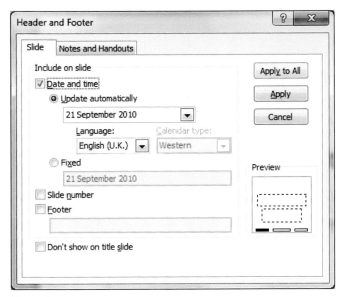

Figure 34

5. The <u>D</u>ate and time facility provides a variety of different formats

6. To update the date automatically, click <u>Update automatically</u>

7. Alternatively choose the required format, click Apply to All

8. This will apply the formats to all the slides including any new slides added

9. To change the font colour or size of the of the date

10. Highlight the date, select Home

11. Click on the downward pointing arrow on the Font Colour icon **A** ▾

12. Select the required colour from the Theme Colours pallet

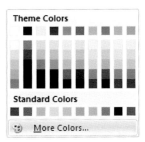

Figure 35

13. Alternatively select More Colours to define a more specific colour

14. Choose a Standard or Custom colour

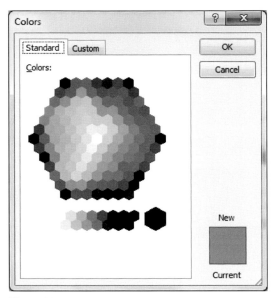

Figure 36

15. Press [OK] to apply the colour in the presentation

Amending Data using the Footer Area

Slide Master allows the user to change the colour, size and style of data used.

1. Click in the footer area, add a company or organisational name
2. If required amend the colour, style and size of the text

Adding a Background Picture

1. Select
2. The Format Background dialog box appears

Figure 37

3. Click on ⊙ Picture or texture fill , select File...

4. Choose the required picture, click Insert ▼

5. Choose Apply to All to add the background to all the slides, or

6. Select Close to apply the background to the current slide

7. Selecting 🎨 Background Styles ▾ , Reset Background resets the background back to white

Colour Schemes

A user can apply a different colour scheme to each individual slide in a presentation however, by editing or selecting a scheme the Master automatically applies the settings to every slide in the presentation.

1. Open a new presentation, select

2. Choose from the Edit Theme Grouping

3. The All Themes gallery appears

Figure 38

4. Select a theme from the Built-In gallery

5. Click on ▦ Colors ▾

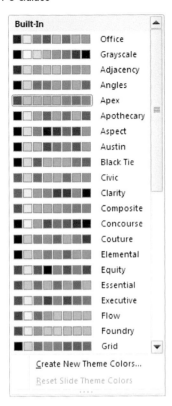

Figure 39

6. Choose the colour theme required

7. Alternatively select [Create New Theme Colors...]

8. The Create New Theme Colours dialog box appears

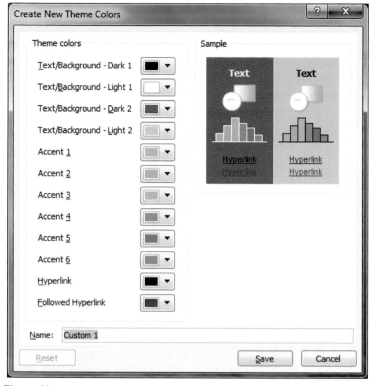

Figure 40

9. Choose the required colours for the pallet, press [Save]

Placeholders

When working in the Slide Master, Handout Master and Notes Master, placeholders appear in the four corners of the slide, these are named the Header Area, Date Area, Footer Area and Number Area.   Think of a placeholder as a named text box, placeholders can be moved to another area or deleted.

Display Handout Master Placeholders

1. Select ⎡ View ⎤ , ⎡ Handout Master ⎤ , the following view is displayed

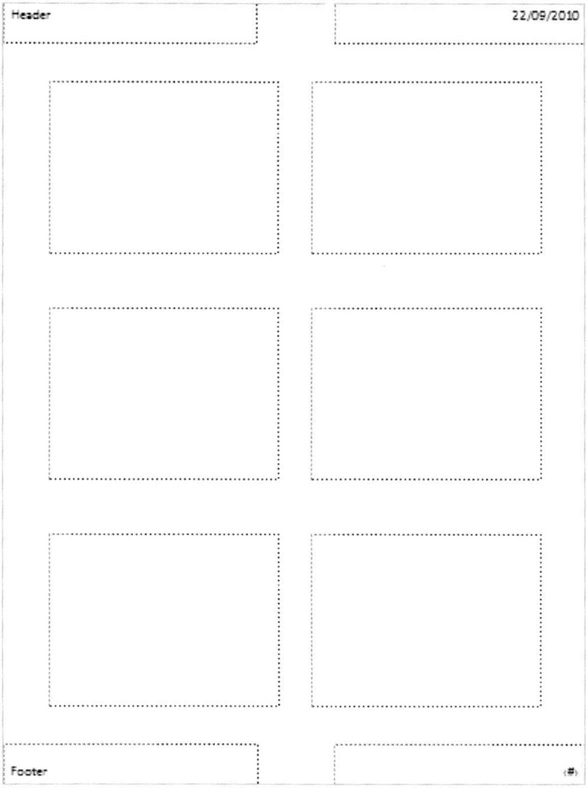

Figure 41

2. Alternatively select Insert , Header & Footer

3. The Header and Footer dialog box appears

4. Select the Notes and Handouts Tab

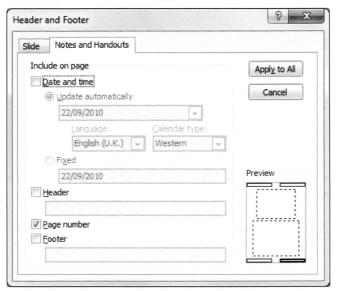

Figure 42

5. Select the required options, press Apply to All

6. Choose File , Print

7. Alternatively press CTRL F2

8. Click with the with the left 🖱 button in the Settings area on Full Page Slides

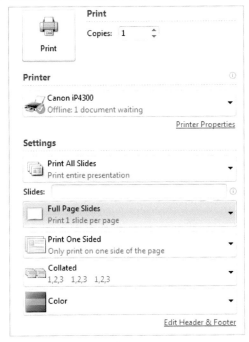

Figure 43

9. Click on the downward pointing arrow on slides to expand the menu

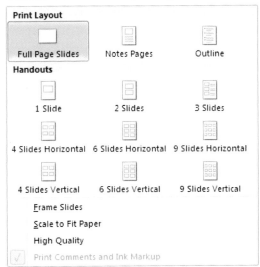

Figure 44

10. Choose the handout option required

11. Alternatively click  View , Handout Master , to display the handout options

12. Select Slides Per Page ▾ , click on the required option

Figure 45

13. Choose Close Master View to return to Normal View

Delete a Placeholder

1. Select click View , Handout Master

2. Remove the ticks from the placeholders not required

☑ Header ☑ Date

☑ Footer ☑ Page Number

Placeholders

Figure 46

3. Choose Close Master View to return to the presentation

4. The placeholder is deleted from the master

Move a Placeholder to a New Location

1. Click with the left  button on the header area in the placeholder

2. The Placeholder is selected

Figure 47

3. Hold the ⌈CTRL⌋ key down, press the appropriate arrow keys ⌈↑⌋
   ⌈↓⌋ ⌈←⌋ ⌈→⌋

4. The placeholder moves to the new destination

Retrieve a Placeholder

1. If the Handout master is not already displayed

2. Choose ⌈View⌋ , ⌈Handout Master⌋

3. Click inside the Handout Master

4. Press the right  button, select ⌈🔲 Handout Master Layout...⌋

Figure 48

5. The placeholders in the active master are highlighted by a tick ☑

6. Click with the left  button to display the ☑Date placeholder

7. Press ⌈ OK ⌋

8. The date placeholder appears in the default position

Exercise 2: - Handout Master

1. Open Creating My First Presentation

2. Display the Handout Master by choosing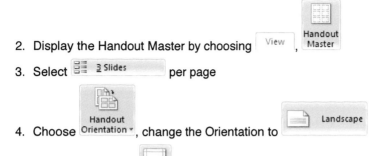

3. Select ⬛ 3 Slides per page

4. Choose 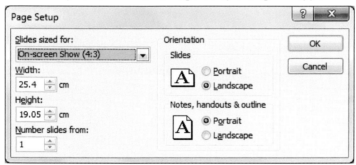, change the Orientation to Landscape

5. Alternatively select 🗔 Page Setup , the Page Setup dialog box appears

6. Set the Orientation to Landscape, click OK

7. Apply a handout background colour of your choice

8. Click in the Header, type Presentation Handout

9. Click in the Footer, type ABC Limited

10. Close Master View

11. Choose File , Print , or press CTRL F2 to preview the results

12. In the Slides area, select

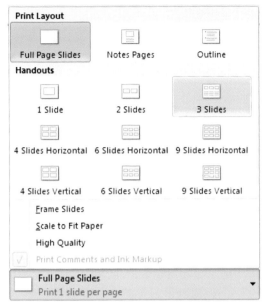

13. The settings area displays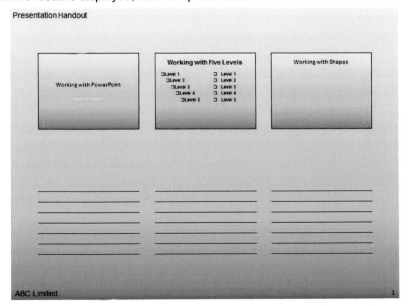

14. The result is displayed, save the presentation

SmartArt

SmartArt allows users to create organisational charts using a variety of shapes. This is useful if a hieratical structure is required.

1. Open a new presentation, select the Title Only slide

2. Click in the title area of the slide, type My Organisational Chart

3. Select  the SmartArt Graphic dialog box appears

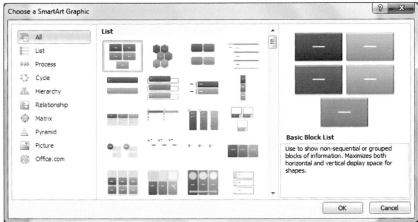

Figure 49

4. Select the category

5. Choose Organisational Chart [image], press [OK]

6. The organisational chart is displayed in the slide

My Organisational Chart

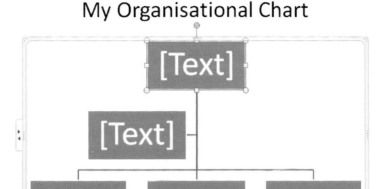

Figure 50

7. Click on the outer edge of the second text box, press [Delete]

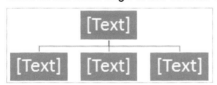

Figure 51

8. Click in the middle text box, press [Delete]

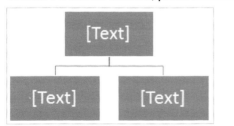

Figure 52

9. Click in the left hand side text box, choose | Design | from SmartArt Tools

10. Select ⬜ Add Shape ˅ , choose 🖬 Add Assistant

11. Repeat steps 9 and 10 to create a second text box

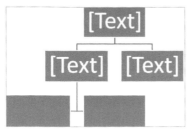

Figure 53

12. Click back in the first text box, type Managing Director

13. The text box will adjust to the appropriate size

14. Alternatively click the left ⌒🖰 button on the arrow ▸◂ on the outline area

15. The following dialog box appears

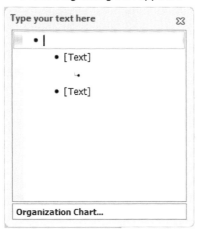

Figure 54

16. Type the text Managing Director, the text box automatically resizes

17. Press the downward arrow key ⬇ to highlight the next text box

Customising Organisational Charts

1. Click in the Managing Director text box

2. Select Colors ▾ to expand the colour gallery

3. Choose a colour of your choice

4. Click on the downward pointing arrow of the SmartArt Styles Grouping

Figure 55

5. Select 3-D

6. Click in a text box, choose Format from

7. Click on the downward pointing arrow of WordArt Styles

Figure 56

8. Choose Gradient Fill - Purple, Accent 4, Reflection

9. To change the colour of the text, select A Text Fill ▾

10. Select A Text Effects ▾ to apply a visual effect to the text

11. Text Outline ▾ changes the colour, width and line style

12. Click on Change Shape ▾ to change the shape of the text box

13. Save the presentation as My First Organisational Chart

Exercise 3: - Organisational Chart

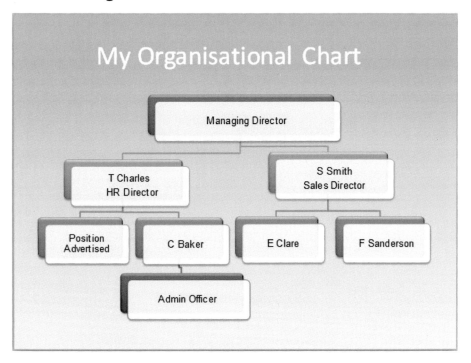

1. Open a new presentation
2. Create an Organisational Chart displaying four levels as shown above
3. Experiment using 3 different styles and colours from the gallery options
4. Apply a style of your choice and save to update the presentation

Outline View

The Outline View is a fast and easy way to create a quick outline for a presentation.

Figure 57

1. Open a new presentation

2. Select the Outline Tab Slides   Outline

3. Click with the left button after the icon 1

4. A flashing cursor is displayed

5. Type Smart PC Guides, the text is inserted into the title slide

6. Press Enter followed by the TAB key, type your name

7. The text appears in the Subtitle area

8. Press Enter, hold down the SHIFT key, press TAB

9. The flashing cursor goes back a level, slide 2 appears

10. Type the heading for the next slide, press Enter

11. Press TAB a bullet appears

12. Type the required list or select the Layout Tab to apply the required style

Exercise 4: - Working in Outline View

The object of this exercise is to create a quick outline for a presentation. If some of the slides need to have a different layout, the layout changes when the appropriate option is selected.

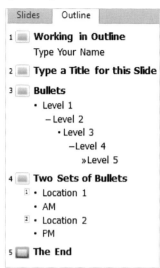

1. Working in Outline View to the left of the screen, type Working in Outline

2. The text appears in the slide and in the outline area

3. Press Enter

4. Press TAB , type your first name and surname

5. Slide 1 is complete

6. Press Enter , hold down SHIFT press TAB , slide 2 text layout appears

7. Insert Type a Title for this Slide, slide 2 is complete

8. Complete the text as displayed above for slide 3

9. Select Home , Layout ▾

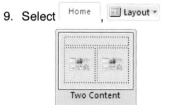

10. Apply   layout to slide 4

© 2010 Voyse Recognition

11. Type the following text

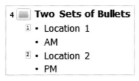

12. To move to column 2, press ⌷ CTRL ⌷ and ⌷ Enter ⌷

13. Complete slide 5

14. Press ⌷ CTRL ⌷ and the ⌷ Home ⌷ key to return to the beginning of the presentation

15. Click on the ⌷ Slide Show ⌷ Tab, use the ⌷ ↓ ⌷ key to run through the slides

16. Select ⌷ CTRL ⌷ ⌷ A ⌷ to highlight all the slides in the presentation

17. Move the mouse pointer ☊ anywhere over the highlighted area in Outline

18. To collapse the slides, click with the right ☝ button, choose

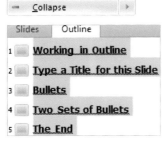

19. To move a slide, collapse the slide, click with the left ☝ button on the slide named Bullets

20. Place the slide named Bullets in the new position as Slide 4

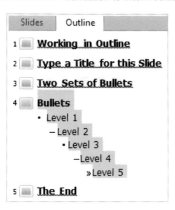

21. Choose the slide named Bullets, right click, press ➕ Expand ▶

22. The text contents have moved, save the presentation as Working in Outline

Slide Sorter View

The Slide Sorter View provides an overall view of all the slides in the presentation and allows slides to be added, repositioned or deleted, as well as displaying transitions, animation effects and timings.

Moving Slides

1. Select View,  Slide Sorter

2. Click with the left ⌒Ö button on the slide to be moved

3. A orange border appears around the selected slide

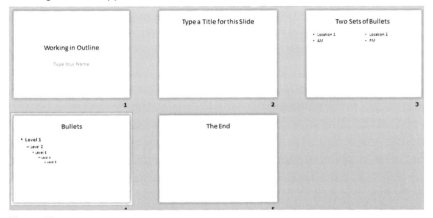

Figure 58

4. Click and hold the left ⌒Ö button down, drag the slide to its new location

5. When the left ⌒Ö button is released the slide is moved to the new location

Deleting Slides

1. Click with the left ⌒Ö button to select the slide to be deleted

2. Press the ⌊Delete⌋ key on the keyboard

Organising Slides into Sections

Applying sections to a presentation is a useful way of organising slides when working with a large presentation.

1. Open the required presentation

2. Select

3. Click with the left 🖱 button where a new section is to appear

4. A black vertical line appears

5. Select

6. Click on ◢ Default Section , select 🗒 Section ▾ , ⬚ Rename Section

7. The Rename Section dialog box appears

8. Rename the Default Section as Section 1, click Rename

Figure 59

9. Repeat the above steps to create additional sections

10. To move a section , click on the section name

11. Click with the right 🖱 button, the section menu is expanded

⬚ Rename Section
🗙 Remove Section
🗙 Remove Section & Slides
🗙 Remove All Sections
▲ Move Section Up
▼ Move Section Down
🗒 Collapse All
🗒 Expand All

Figure 60

12. Select  or ▼ Move Section Down

13. To remove the sections, select 🗙 Remove All Sections

14. To remove the section and slides, select 🗙 Remove Section & Slides

15. To collapse or expand the sections, select ▷ Collapse All or

🔼 Expand All

Insert a Video or Audio into a Presentation

Videos and audios can be inserted into a presentation by inserting them from a file or the Clip Art task pane by inserting them as objects. Once the video or audio has been installed it can be played back using the playback bar or the playback tab under the Video and Audio Tools Grouping.

Inserting a Video or Audio from a File

1. Open the required presentation, select where the video or audio clip is to appear

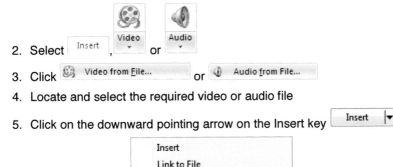

2. Select Insert , Video ▼ or Audio ▼

3. Click 🎞 Video from File... or 🔊 Audio from File...

4. Locate and select the required video or audio file

5. Click on the downward pointing arrow on the Insert key [Insert ▼]

   Insert
   Link to File
   Show previous versions

6. Select Link to File

7. The video or audio clip appears in the presentation

8. The video appears as part of the presentation

9. The audio clip appears as a small icon representing the sound 🔊

Playing a Video

1. Select the video, press the Play/Pause button

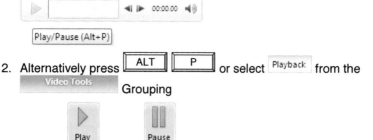

2. Alternatively press ALT P or select Playback from the Video Tools Grouping

3. Choose Preview , select Preview to pause the video

4. To move forward or backward click the buttons on the playback bar

5. To change the volume select the mute/unmute button

Playing an Audio Clip

1. Select the audio clip in the presentation

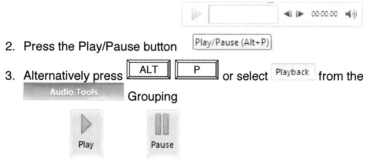

2. Press the Play/Pause button   Play/Pause (Alt+P)

3. Alternatively press ALT P or select Playback from the Audio Tools Grouping

4. Choose Preview , select Preview to pause the audio clip

5. To move forward or backward click the buttons on the playback bar

6. To change the volume select the mute/unmute button

Working with Graphics

Presentations can be enhanced and made more interesting by inserting graphics, drawing objects, pictures, charts or text and then by grouping, scaling, cropping or re-colouring the graphics.

Inserting Clip Art in a Slide

1. Add a new Title Only slide

2. Select ⌷ Insert ⌷ , ⌷ Clip Art ⌷ , the Clip Art dialog box appears

Figure 61

3. In the Search for: box type Business, press ⌷ Go ⌷

4. The Clip Art dialog box shows the results

5. Use the scroll bar to view the options

6. Click on the ▾ arrow on the picture, select ⌷ Insert ⌷

Figure 62

7. The picture is displayed in the slide

8. To delete the picture, click in the picture with the left ⌒🖱 button

9. Press ▣ Delete ▣

Edit a Picture in a Slide

1. Click on the picture

Figure 63

2. Move the mouse pointer ⬉ over the sizing handles, drag to edit the picture

3. To move the picture to another position, click in the picture and drag

4. To rotate the picture, click in the picture, the | Picture Tools Format | Tab appears

5. Select | Format |, choose ◩ Rotate ▾ from the Format Arrange Grouping

6. Move the mouse pointer ⬉ over the options to show how the picture looks

Figure 64

7. Select ◩ Flip Horizontal

8. Move the mouse pointer ⬉ to a green circle ○, a black circular arrow appears

9. Click and hold down the left ⌒🖱 button, drag to rotate to the required position

Figure 65

Cropping Pictures

The Picture Tools option appears when a picture is selected in a slide.

1. Click the left button on the **Picture Tools** Format Tab to display the Picture Tools

2. Select a picture by using the left button

Figure 66

3. Click the Crop icon  from the Picture Tools

Figure 67

4. Move over a black handle

5. Drag over the area that needs to be taken out

6. Repeat the process until you see the tiger's face

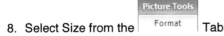

Figure 68

7. Press the left button and drag to hide the information not required

8. Select Size from the **Picture Tools** Format Tab

Figure 69

9. Click the arrows in the height and width area to increase or decrease the size

10. Expand the Size Grouping by clicking on , the Layout dialog box appears

11. Ensure the Size Tab is selected

12. Alternatively select the picture to be resized

13. Right 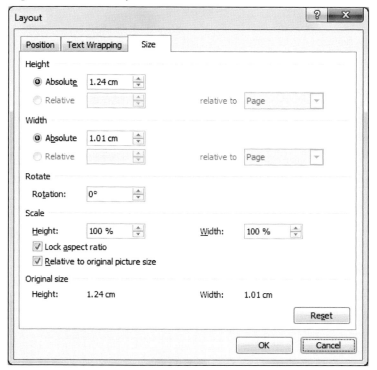 click on the picture select ⊞ Si̱ze and Position...

Figure 70

14. In the Scale area, amend the **H**eight and **W**idth to 300%

15. Click [OK]

Removing a Picture Background

1. Click in the picture where the background is to be removed

Figure 71

2. Select   , the background area is highlighted

Figure 72

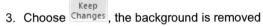

3. Choose   , the background is removed

Figure 73

Inserting WordArt

1. To insert text as an object, select [Insert] ,

2. The WordArt Gallery appears

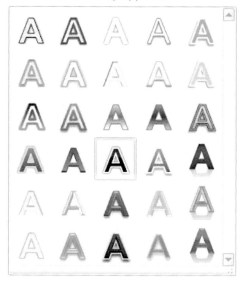

Figure 74

3. Select a style to appear in the slide

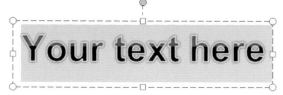

Figure 75

4. Type the required text

Figure 76

5. The Drawing Tools Tab appears  in the Ribbon

6. Click on **Text Effects ▾** in the WordArt Styles Grouping

7. Choose **3-D Rotation ▸** , select Perspective Right

Smart PC Guides

Figure 77

Adding Shadows

1. Select **Shape Effects ▾**, **Shadow ▸** from the Shape Styles

2. Choose Perspective Diagonal Upper Left

Smart PC Guides

Figure 78

Edit WordArt

1. Click with the left 🖰 button on the text to be edited

2. Edit text as required

Formatting WordArt in a Document

1. To change the colour of the WordArt, select the text to be changed

2. Click **A Text Fill ▾**, choose the required colour

Smart PC Guides

Figure 79

AutoShapes

Ready-made basic shapes, for example rectangles, circles, block arrows, flowcharts, symbols, banners and callouts can be added to slides to enhance its appearance.

1. Select **Insert** , **Shapes** from the Illustrations Grouping

2. The Shapes gallery appears, choose Callouts

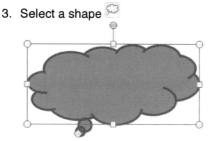

Figure 80

3. Select a shape

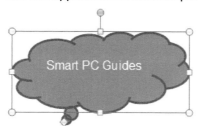

Figure 81

4. Drag in the slide for the AutoShape to appear

5. Type the text required in the AutoShape

6. The text appears in the AutoShape in the slide

Figure 82

7. Click the downward arrow to reveal more options

Shape Fill ▾
Shape Outline ▾
Shape Effects ▾

Shape Styles

Figure 83

8. Select Intense Effect, Orange, Accent 6

Figure 84

Drawing Tools

1. To use a drawing object, select Line ⟍ from the Shapes gallery

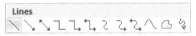

Figure 85

2. Hold down the left button and drag

3. Click back on the Line icon ⟍

4. Position the mouse pointer on the circle next to the line and drag

Figure 86

5. Repeat the above steps to complete the required shape

6. To draw a shape, click on the shape from the Shapes gallery

7. Move the mouse pointer where the object is to appear

8. Hold down the left button and drag, release the mouse button

9. Repeat the process to create as many shapes as required

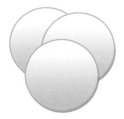

Figure 87

Drawing Objects from a Central Point

1. Click in the slide where the object is to appear
2. Select an object from the Shapes gallery using the left  button
3. Press and hold down the ⬚Shift key, drag the object onto the page
4. Release the mouse button before the ⬚Shift key
5. Click outside the drawing box

Figure 88

6. To add a 3-D effect, select the object
7. Select ⬚Format from the Drawing Tools Tab

8. Click on , choose Pre-set 9

Figure 89

9. To format the 3-D Shape
10. Select ⬚ Shape Effects ▾, ⬚ Preset ▸, 🔧 3-D Options...
11. The Format Shape dialog box appears
12. Click ⬚ Close to return to the document

Drawing a Text Box

Text boxes allow text to be positioned anywhere in a slide.

1. To insert a text box, select

2. Select Draw Text Box

3. Click where you want to start the text box, drag to the required size

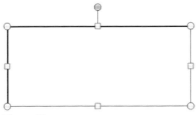

Figure 90

4. Type inside the box to add text

5. To move the text box, click on the edge of the box

6. Use the arrow keys ↓ ↑ → ← to move the text box to the new position

7. Alternatively click with the left button on the edge of the text box and drag

8. Release the mouse when the text box is in its new location

9. To delete a box, position the mouse pointer over the edge of the text box

10. A four headed arrow appears, click on the border, press Delete

Inserting Objects

1. Add a Title Slide to your presentation

2. Select | Insert | Object ,

3. Click with the left 🖱 button on Create from file, choose Browse... , select the file

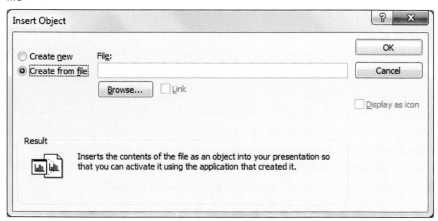

Figure 91

4. Read the Result in the screen print preview area

5. Click the Link icon ☑ Link to review the revised results

6. This enables changes in the file to be reflected in the slide

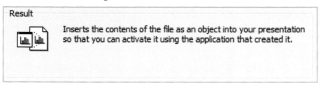

Figure 92

7. Click OK , the object appears in the presentation

Linked Information

If changes have been made to a linked object when the PowerPoint file is opened, select **U**pdate Links to add the latest image of the object.

Exercise 5: - Drawing Shapes

1. Open a new presentation
2. Select a blank layout slide
3. Insert an Oval shape
4. Move the mouse pointer ⬫ into the slide a black hairline cross appears
5. Click with the left ⬫ button, the selected shape is displayed
6. Alternatively click and drag in the slide to the desired size for the shape
7. Produce the following slide

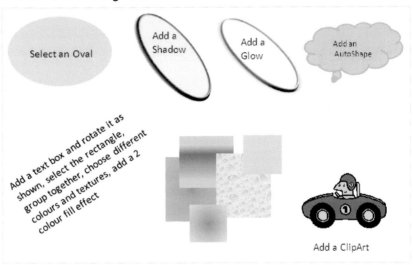

8. Save the slide

Chart Layout Feature

PowerPoint allows you to create a chart or import a Microsoft Excel worksheet or chart. You can enter your own data on the datasheet, import data from a text file, or paste data from another program.

The advantage of working with the chart layout slide is that information can be presented graphically on one slide making it is easier to understand. In slide layout there are a number of different ways to display a chart, an example of the four most popular styles are displayed below:

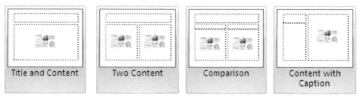

| Title and Content | Two Content | Comparison | Content with Caption |

Figure 93

1. Select a new presentation, choose a slide containing a chart feature

2. Click with the left button on the chart icon to add the chart to the slide

3. The Insert Chart dialog box appears

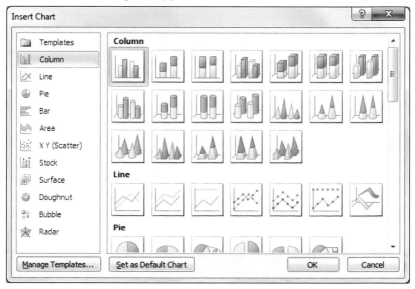

Figure 94

© 2010 Voyse Recognition

4. Select

5. Click [OK]

6. The window splits to show the PowerPoint slide and the Excel data

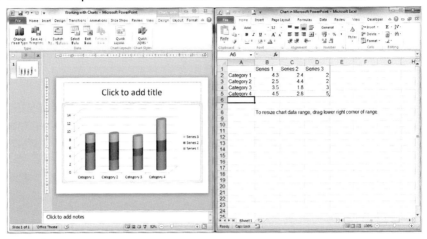

Figure 95

7. Using the Excel sheet change or update the data as required

8. Click outside the data area

9. Click into the PowerPoint slide, the chart is updated automatically

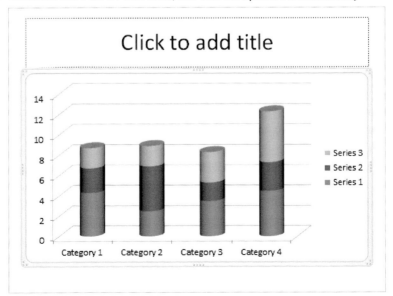

Figure 96

10. To edit the data click in the chart, select **Edit Data** to bring back the Excel data sheet

11. Edit the data and close the Excel screen

12. The data is updated in the chart

13. To change the colour scheme in the chart, click in the chart area

14. Select the **Design** Tab, choose **Colors ▾** to expand the colour gallery

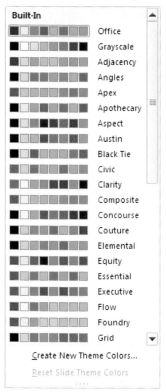

Figure 97

15. Use the mouse pointer to move over the different colour schemes

16. The different colour schemes are shown on the slide

17. Click to select the required colour scheme

18. To change the chart type, click in the chart area

19. Select Chart Type , the Change Chart Type dialog box appears

20. Choose ⊕ Pie , Exploded pie in 3-D  , press OK

Figure 98

21. To rotate data in the chart, click in the chart area

22. Select Layout from the Chart Tools area

23. Select 3-D Rotation , the Format Chart Area dialog box appears

Figure 99

24. Use the arrows to change the rotation

25. Press [Close], the slide is updated, save the presentation

Inserting Tables into a Presentation

PowerPoint presents a number of different ways to display a table in a presentation, an example of the four most popular styles are displayed below:

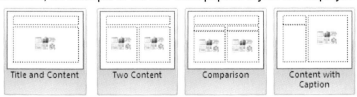

Figure 100

1. Select a new presentation, choose a slide containing a table feature
2. Click with the left 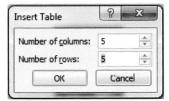 the table icon
3. The Insert Table dialog box appears

Figure 101

4. Select the number of columns and rows required, click OK

5. Alternatively choose Insert , Table

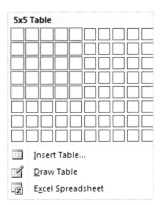

Figure 102

6. Highlight the required number of columns and rows
7. Press the left button, the table is inserted into the slide

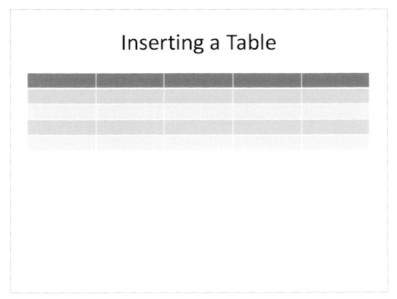

Figure 103

Table Formatting

1. Click in the table, choose [Design] from the [Table Tools] Grouping

2. Select ☑ Banded Rows to display even rows differently from odd rows to make reading the table easier, or select the required table style option

☐ Header Row	☐ First Column
☐ Total Row	☐ Last Column
☐ Banded Rows	☐ Banded Columns

Table Style Options

Figure 104

3. To change the visual style of the table, select [Design]

4. Click on the downward pointing arrow on the Table Styles Grouping

Figure 105

5. Select the required style

Running a Slide Show

PowerPoint enables a presentation to be run through a projector as a slide show. It could, for example be used to promote a new product in the form of a presentation from a Reception area, in this example timing and transitions would be applied to the presentation to attract the attention of both staff and visitors who could view information on the new product.

Another example may require the presenter to progress to the next slide when they are ready; therefore timings would not be required in this form of delivery. In both examples the slides may contain transitions and build effects to enhance the presentation.

1. Open the presentation My First Presentation, click on the first slide

2. Choose Slide Show , choose From Beginning, alternatively press F5

3. Click with the left button to display the second slide

4. Repeat the process for the rest of the slides

5. Alternatively use ← → ↑ ↓ , press F1 to learn more on Slide Show options

6. To exit Slide Show press the ESC key on the keyboard

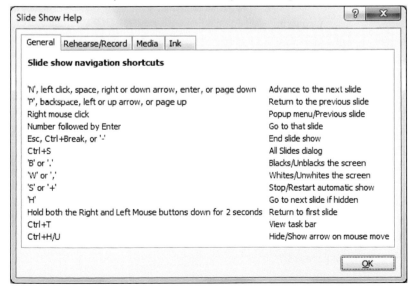

Figure 106

Hide/Unhide Slides

Presentations can be delivered to a different audience by hiding slides that are not relevant to that audience.

1. Open a presentation, select View , Slide Sorter

2. Move the mouse pointer ᛣ over the slide to be hidden

3. Click with the right ᴃ button, choose ◩ Hide Slide

4. A diagonal line is displayed through the chosen slide ◩

5. The slide will not be displayed when running a presentation using the slide show

6. To Unhide the slide move the mouse pointer ᛣ over the hidden slide

7. Click with the right ᴃ button, choose ◩ Hide Slide

8. The normal slide number is displayed **1**

9. Alternatively select Slide Show , Hide Slide

Slide Transitions

Transition effects can be added to a presentation to enhance the visual appearance of a slide(s).

1. Select Transitions

2. Click on the downward ▾ arrow from the Transition To This Slide Grouping

Figure 107

3. The gallery is expanded

4. Move the mouse pointer ᛣ over the designs to see how they appear in the presentation

5. Choose the required transition Ferris Wheel

6. To add sound to the transition, select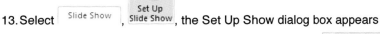

7. Using the downward pointing arrow ⌄ select the sound required

8. If the sound needs to be applied to all the slides select ≡↲ Apply To All

Rehearse Timings

PowerPoint allows timings to be set in presentations.

1. Select the first slide in the slide show

2. Click on Slide Show , choose Rehearse Timings

3. The presentation is displayed with the Rehearsal counter

    Figure 108

4. The ⇨ icon when selected displays the next slide

5. The ‖ icon is used to pause the time of the presentation

6. The 0:00:06 displays the individual slide time

7. The Repeat icon ↻ restarts the individual slide to zero seconds

8. The last information area 0:00:15 displays the combined time of all the slides

9. At the end of all the slides a prompt appears

    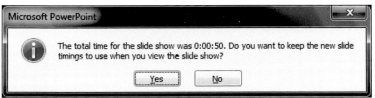

    Microsoft PowerPoint

    The total time for the slide show was 0:00:50. Do you want to keep the new slide timings to use when you view the slide show?

    [Yes]   [No]

    Figure 109

10. To keep the new slide timings select Yes , alternatively choose No

11. Turning off timings does not delete them

12. Turn them back on at any time without having to recreate them

13. Select Slide Show , Set Up Slide Show , the Set Up Show dialog box appears

14. To turn timings on select the Advance slide box choose ⦿ Using timings, if present

15. To turn timings off select the Advance slide box choose ⊙ Manually

16. Press [OK] to return to the presentation

This concludes the PowerPoint 2010 Foundation to Intermediate Guide. Thank you for choosing Smart PC Guides, we look forward to your continued use of Smart PC Guides. For a comprehensive view of our guides please visit our website www.smart-pc-guides.com

© 2010 Voyse Recognition

Shortcut Keys

SHORTCUT KEYS		DESCRIPTION	SHORTCUT KEYS			DESCRIPTION
CTRL	F1	Display or Hide the Ribbon	ALT	F	P	Displays Print Dialog Box
CTRL	B	Apply or Remove Bold Format	ALT	H	I	New Slide Options
CTRL	C	Copy Selected Information	ALT	V	I	Grid/Guides Dialog Box
CTRL	P	Displays Print Dialog Box	ALT	W	M	Slide Master Options
CTRL	S	Saves the Presentation	ALT	W	R	Display or Hide the Ruler
CTRL	U	Apply or Remove Underline	CTRL	SHIFT	P	Displays Font Dialog Box
CTRL	V	Paste Selected Information				
CTRL	X	Cuts Selected Information				
CTRL	Y	Repeats Previous Command				
CTRL	Z	Undo Previous Command				
CTRL	F2	Displays Print Preview				
SHIFT	F3	Upper, Lower or Initial Caps				
F1		PowerPoint Help				
F5		Starts Slide Show				
F7		Spell Checker				
F12		Save As Dialog Box				

Index